KT-566-753

Being a
DJ

Kathy Galashan

Published in association with The Basic Skills Agency

Hodder & Stoughton

A MEMBER OF THE HODDER HEADLINE GROUP

Acknowledgements

Cover: Getty Images/Photodisc

Photos: p 1 Sally and Richard Greenhill; pp 3, 11 A Medley/SIN; p 6 Melanie Cox/SIN; p 15 Popperfoto; p18 Richard Fawcett/SIN; p 23 Martyn Goodacre/SIN

Every effort has been made to trace copyright holders of material reproduced in this book. Any rights not acknowledged will be acknowledged in subsequent printings if notice is given to the publisher.

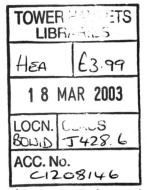
Orders; please contact Bookpoint Ltd, 130 Milton Park, Abingdon, Oxon OX14 4SB. Telephone: (44) 01235 827720, Fax: (44) 01235 400454. Lines are open from 9.00–6.00, Monday to Saturday, with a 24 hour message answering service. You can also order through our website: www.hodderheadline.co.uk

British Library Cataloguing in Publication Data
A catalogue record for this title is available from the British Library

ISBN 0 340 87694 8

First published 2000
This edition published 2002
Impression number   10 9 8 7 6 5 4 3 2 1
Year   2007 2006 2005 2004 2003 2002

Copyright © 2000 Kathy Galashan

Typeset by SX Composing DTP, Rayleigh, Essex.
Printed in Great Britain for Hodder and Stoughton Educational, 338 Euston Road, London NW1 3BH, by The Bath Press Ltd, Bath.

Contents

I'm Jack.
I love music –
loud music
with a strong beat.
I want to make money
doing something I love.
Music is my thing and
I want to make money from music.
I'm going to find out about being a DJ.

A volunteer DJ for a hospital radio.

I'm Tod.
I work four days a week
in a record shop.
On Fridays and Saturdays
I play at clubs.
I love being a DJ.
Everyone remembers music.
The great track.
The tune that's playing
the night you meet someone special.
DJs make memories.
They make the rave
and the big hit.

A DJ playing in a nightclub.

First Things First

Tod OK. Why do you want to be a DJ?

Jack I love music.
I've got stacks of CDs.
I play them all the time.

Tod What music do you like?
You need to know what sort of DJ
you want to be.

Jack Most of the time
I listen to hip hop and dance.
I like reggae, too.

Tod That's fine.
That's a good scene for a DJ.
You can be a hip hop or dance DJ
or you can collect different music.

Jack Can you make money as a DJ?

Tod It's hard at the beginning.
No one pays a new DJ much.
Most start doing it for free
or for a few drinks.

I get paid for my gigs
but not enough to live off.
Some DJs are millionaires.
It takes time and luck.

Take Carl Cox.
He's very rich indeed.
He's a black British DJ
and plays dance music.
He plays clubs all over the world
and makes records.

Carl Cox

Jack So what do I need to do?

Tod You need three things –
music,
equipment, and
a place to play.

And luck as well.
You need luck to get a break,
to get started.

Music

Jack Let's start with music.
What do I need?

Tod You know what you like,
that's a start.
You need lots of CDs and records.

You can buy them
or borrow them off friends.

A good thing is to keep up with new tunes.
You want the newest tunes to play.

Equipment

Jack What about equipment?

Tod When I started
I hired the basics.
Hiring equipment
costs about £150 a night now.
The clubs and pubs I play at
normally have a PA system set up.
That means all the equipment is there
for you to use.

Jack What are the basics?
How much are they to buy?

Tod Two decks,
one or two CD players,
a mixer,
an amp,
speakers.
Even a cheap outfit can cost
more than £1,000.

I don't think it's worth it for clubs.
You buy something
and then tomorrow you see something
better and cheaper.

You can always hire
anything you need.

A basic outfit includes decks and mixers.

Jack What about lights and videos and screens –
all the things that make a great night?

Tod You can hire anything, but it costs.
Usually clubs have their own equipment.

And don't forget transport.
With equipment you need a car, van or taxi
to get you there and home again.

A Place to Play

Jack How do I get a place to play at?

Tod There are different sorts of DJs.
Some play in raves.
Some play at clubs and pubs.
Some play on the radio.

You can't start at the top.
Have you ever tried being a DJ?

Jack I did a wedding
for a mate in a local pub.

I go to college one day a week.
On Saturdays it's club night
and I talk to the DJ there.
Sometimes he lets me
do the first 30 minutes.

Tod You're on your way.
Can you do a club night
when he's away?

Talk to people.
Tell them you want to play.
Try new clubs
and tell them you've got experience.

If you can,
tape yourself being a DJ.
Then leave a copy of the demo
with the client
so they can hear what you're like.

Simon Dee, a famous DJ from the 1960s. He worked for
Radio Caroline.

Look out for new local clubs and pubs.
Get to them before they hire a full-time DJ.
Local papers are good for finding out things.
It's about checking out what's happening
and being there.

For hip hop or dance,
try a local radio station.
The first pirate radio station
was Radio Caroline
which was broadcast from a ship.

Pirate stations often give local people
a break.
Phone up and send a demo tape.

The Rave

Jack What happens at a rave?

Tod At a rave, thousands of people
come to dance and have a good time.

Before I go, I choose what I want
and pack my cases.
I make sure I've got the right CDs and
records.

When I get there
everything is already set up.
I have to be ready
to fit in with the other DJs.
It's up to me to keep the rave going.

Working at the Ministry of Sound.

A good night is a night
when everyone dances.
Some tunes fill the floor –
and others empty it.
Every night is different.

At raves I play with other DJs.
I normally play for an hour or two.

At a club I may play the whole set –
five or six hours.

I can get £150 to £200 on a good night.
Famous DJs can get thousands.

DJ Skills

Jack Different DJs can play the same tracks
but make them sound different.

Tod Yes, it's what DJs do to tracks
that makes the sound.
They mix records.
You need two decks and a mixer.
Play one record over the amp.
Listen to the second one on headphones.
Use the fader
to move from one deck to another.

That's how you can make music
carry on without a break.

You can cut from one tune to another
and back again.

You can play one tune over another.
It all makes the same record sound different.

Scratching is another trick.

Put a record on the deck.
Put the needle in the groove
and spin the record
backwards and forwards.
Then a new sound comes out
and you can mix this with other tunes.

Some DJs have an MC, a front person,
chatting over the tracks
to keep the ravers lively.
It gets people going.

Radio DJ

Jack What about the radio?
I'd like to be a radio DJ.

Tod You need to be upfront.
A showman.
A performer.
Good DJs talk to the audience
and introduce records.
They are quick.
they know what people like
and can put on a good show.

Jack I can do that.
I'm never stuck for words.
I make my friends laugh.

Tod Make a demo tape.
Send it to a local radio station.
Sometimes colleges, hospitals
and shopping centres have radio stations.
Talk to people, give out demo tapes
and hope you get lucky.

Radio One DJs Steve Lamacq and Jo Whiley.

Types of Music

Hip Hop

Dance

Rap

Techno

Reggae

Blues

Soul

R & B

House

Disco

Garage

Drum n Base

Jungle

Big Beat

Finding Out More

Read listings in newspapers and magazines
such as *Time Out* and the *Big Issue*.
Local papers and free papers
have local ads and news.

Black Music

Echoes is a weekly paper
with news and listings.
Touch is a monthly magazine.
Blues & Soul comes out every two weeks.

To hire equipment

Look in the *Yellow Pages* under 'Disco – Mobile'.

Use the Internet

Look up D.J. Rhythms WWW Links Catalog.

http:/www.djrhythms.com/links/

This is a page that connects you
to information about artists, clubs, record labels,
equipment, and magazines.

Many record labels have their own web site.

Special courses

Some colleges run studio skills courses.

They show how to set up equipment and use it.

Ask at your local careers centre.

Glossary of Terms Used

Amp Equipment that makes the music louder

Deck Equipment used to play records

Demo A tape or CD that you make to show what you can do

DJ Someone who plays records and music in public. They choose what to play and how it is played

Gig A show

Mixer Equipment a DJ uses that lets him or her control the sounds they are playing

MC A presenter who talks to the audience

PA The loud speakers or sound system

Pirate station An illegal radio station. People set up a radio station without a licence